Biscuit Tin Genie

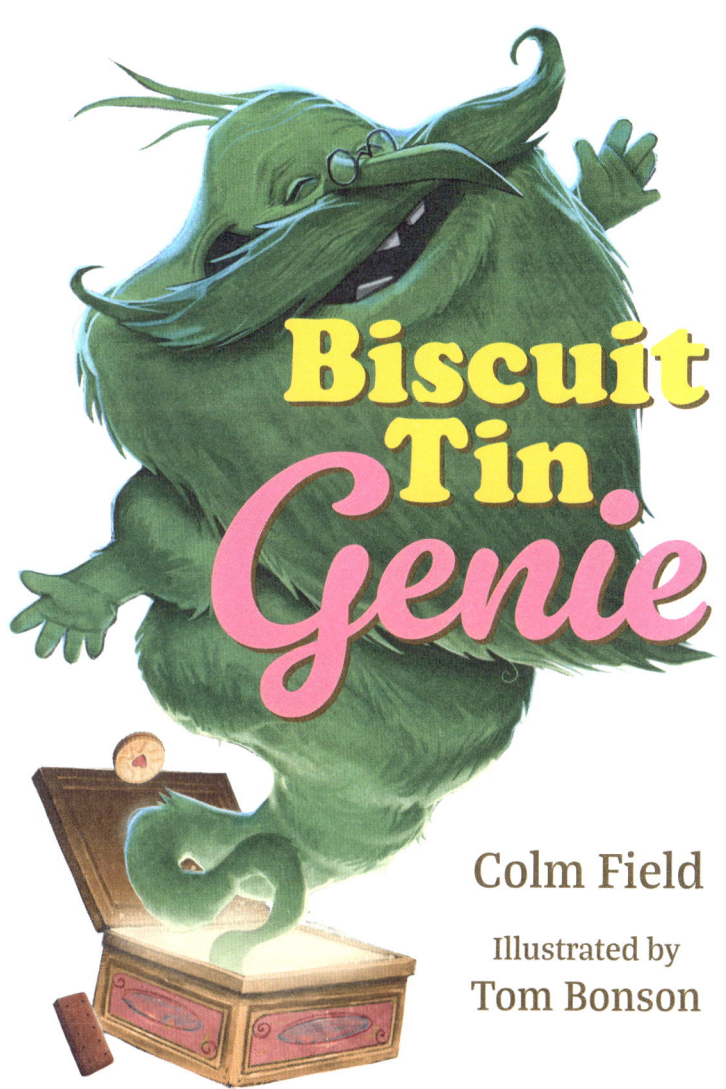

Biscuit Tin Genie

Colm Field

Illustrated by
Tom Bonson

Collins

Contents

Bonus The most incredible
   second-hand finds 6

Chapter 1 9

Bonus Genies and Pookas 22

Chapter 2 25

Bonus Bizarre sports day 40

Chapter 3 43

Bonus Party checklist 56

Chapter 4 59

Bonus Map of Jennifer's town 72

Chapter 5 75

Chapter 6 91

Bonus Pol's favourite wishes 104

About the author 106

About the illustrator 108

Book chat 110

Bonus

The most incredible second-hand finds

At a charity shop or a car boot sale, on the internet or even in the sea, people are always finding treasures that are worth more than you would ever believe.

In Wales, a woman bought a 'toy' ring for her daughter from a charity shop. It turned out to contain a real Russian diamond.

In 2006, in the Philippines, a fisherman found a rock in the sea. It turned out to be the world's biggest pearl.

In 2006, in Germany, a woman bought a sofa from a flea market, and found a painting inside that was 400 years old.

In 1989, in the US, a man bought a painting and found a piece of paper in the frame. It was the Declaration of Independence, one of the US's most important documents ever.

And in England, a girl named Jennifer Jones bought a genie lamp from a car boot sale. Here's what she found …

Chapter 1

Jennifer Jones's life was a crushing disappointment when compared to Casey's.

It wouldn't be so bad, if only she could win the sprint race at sports day like Casey. Or if she could have a *proper* birthday party, like Casey's, with a disco and ketchup in little pots. If she had a big house like Casey, with lots of rooms and even more toys, then her life would be *great*. But she didn't. Jennifer's life was basically a disaster.

Fortunately, there was a solution. And Jennifer was sure this solution could be found at the car boot sale.

Have you ever been to a car boot sale? They're amazing: table after table of people selling second-hand toys, clothes, even old magazines. It's like an Aladdin's cave of treasure, which is funny, considering what Jennifer was looking for.

"I, Jennifer Jones," she whispered, as she walked between the stalls, "am going to find a jinn."

Ever since reading a book called *One Thousand and One Nights*, Jennifer had learned everything about genies. She knew they weren't actually called 'genies' but 'jinn'. She knew they were trapped in ancient ornate oil lamps that looked like teapots. She knew that a jinn gave you three wishes, but that if you were clever, you could trick them into giving you four, *and*, if you used your last wish to set the jinn free, you would have a wish-giving friend forever.

It was simple. All she needed was the right lamp.

"Not you again!" the grizzly old man cried, as she approached his stall.

Jennifer grinned. Old Shay was a grumpy old man, even her dad said so. But his stall contained wonders. There were thick rugs woven from a hundred bright colours. There were gleaming statuettes, the kind that spring to life at midnight. And there were lamps. Glimmering brass lamps that might have been forged in the mythical King Solomon's mines. Lamps that beg you to rub them … until you leap back in shock as smoke pours out and a booming voice declares: **You have released the mighty Jinn! Your wish is my command!**

"Hey up, Shay," Jennifer said. "You having a good boot?"

"Good?" Old Shay groaned. "How can it be good, standing on my bad feet all day? Why on earth are you here, anyway?"

"I'm looking for – "

"I know what you're looking for," he grumbled. "Another blimmin' lamp. You'll wish yer life away."

Jennifer didn't really understand what Old Shay meant, but she'd stopped listening anyway. There, tucked at the back of the table, between an old music box and a model of the solar system, was a lamp she'd never seen before.

"That's new." The lamp she was pointing at was a *proper* oil lamp, with a long, curved spout, and a round lid in the middle. Its beautiful golden burnish was as deep as volcano embers, and when Jennifer lifted it, she was astonished how heavy it felt. It was almost like something was hiding inside.

"How much is it?" she asked.

"I can't keep taking your money like this, Jennifer, it's just a lamp."

"How much, Shay?"

"I cleaned it an' everything. No genie came out, I promise you."

"How. Much?"

Old Shay sighed. "Are you never going to stop looking for a genie?" he asked. Jennifer shook her head. He looked away, as though deciding on something. Then, at last, he picked up the lamp.

"Yessss!" Jennifer said. "Thanks, Old Shay!" She held out her chore money, the crisp ten pound note she'd worked so hard for, but the elderly man shook his head.

"No charge," he said bitterly.

"But – "

"No charge!" Shay snapped, in a voice so fierce, she didn't dare argue. And then he did something even stranger. Instead of just handing the lamp over, he crouched down and picked up, of all things, a biscuit tin. He tucked the lamp inside it.

It was an old tin, old like the lamp but in a different way: a *useful* type of old. The tin had once been a deep red, but now it was covered in scratches and dents, shiny metal lines like earthquake cracks. The picture on the lid showed a faded collection of old-fashioned biscuits – chocolate bourbons, custard creams, and treats she'd never seen before. But whatever company had made these treats, it hadn't been very good at advertising, because there was no name on them at all.

"So you don't scratch it, see?" said Shay. Jennifer was about to object that the lamp would more likely scratch rattling around in the tin … but when she lifted it, nothing moved inside at all.

"Thank you," she said. She really meant it, too.

"Hmph," he replied. "Don't say I didn't warn you." It was only later that she thought that was a strange thing to say.

※

The rest of the day crawled by. Jennifer had never wanted Sunday to be over so fast! At last, she said goodnight to Dad and his girlfriend, Heidi, and hurried to her bedroom. The biscuit tin was still where she'd left it, on her rug. Jennifer lifted the lid, took out the lamp, and held her breath. This was it.

She rubbed the lamp.

Pause.

Nothing happened.

She rubbed the lamp again.

"Jinn, come out!"

Still nothing happened. Jennifer rubbed it again, this time with her T-shirt. Soon the antique looked shiny and new.

And still, no jinn appeared.

Jennifer sat back, her heart heavy. She'd been so certain *this* lamp would contain a jinn! Now her idea seemed silly. There would be no big house. No big birthday party. No sports day success.

Fighting back tears, she put the lamp in her old toybox. The box was *packed* with old lamps, and Jennifer had no idea what to do with them. The grubby old biscuit tin lay open on the floor, and as she shut the lid, she felt a sudden burst of anger. Her life was *so* unfair.

"Stupid tin," she snarled. "Stupid lamps, stupid –" and she pounded the lid with her fist.

"Ouch!"

Jennifer froze. Slowly, she removed her fist from the dented tin lid. Had somebody just spoken?

"Hello?" she said, but there was no answer. She tried to lift the lid, but she had punched it down tight, and it wouldn't budge. So, she rapped it with her knuckles again.

"OUCH!!!"

The lid fired off the box, followed by billowing clouds of smoke that smelled *awful*. An enormous figure emerged, and Jennifer flung herself back, bracing herself for the booming, threatening voice of the jinn saying something like: ***WHO DARES DISTURB THE SLEEP OF THE MIGHTY JINN?!***

But no bellow came. Eventually, Jennifer opened her eyes. And stared.

The figure had shrunk. It floated just above the ground, its head no higher than Jennifer's hips. It looked furry, but its 'fur' was a swirling green mist, and Jennifer suspected that if she dared to touch it, her fingers would brush nothing but damp fog. Its green face looked like it had been drawn by a toddler. The foul-smelling smoke cleared, and the figure looked around.

Then it sniffed. "It stinks in here," it said loudly. "Was that you?"

Bonus

Genies and Pookas

Genies, also called Jinn, or Djinn, are mythical spirits who grant your wishes.

Some of the most famous Jinn can be found in *One Thousand and One Nights*, an ancient collection of stories from the Middle East.

But Jinn are not the only wish-granting creatures. In Irish mythology, Pooka, also called Puca or Puck, are mythical spirits, who *might* grant your wishes … or might not.

Pookas have been in Irish fairy tales for over a thousand years!

Chapter 2

"Who are you?" Jennifer said, astonished.

The figure tutted, like that was a silly question. "Who am I?" he scoffed. He sounded like a 'he' anyway. "I'm Pol, of course! Pol, the great and wise – "

Pol's introduction was ruined when a wisp of smoke entered his mouth. At once he began to cough, dramatically and *much* too loudly.

"You all right, Jen?" a voice called from the living room. It was Heidi, her dad's girlfriend. Heidi was lovely. She worked at a pastry shop and was always bringing treats back. But even she wouldn't be happy about this strange spluttering figure in their flat.

"I'm fine, just a cough!" Jennifer called back. "*Shhh!*" she hissed to Pol. "*You'll get us caught!*"

"Caught?" Pol said, *still* too loudly. "I haven't done anything wrong, thank you very – "

Before he could finish, the bedroom door opened. Jennifer whirled around, looking *very* guilty.

"Heidi!" she said.

She'd expected a yell of alarm at the sight of Pol. But Heidi smiled.

"Any luck with your new lamp?"

"Er … no." It wasn't *exactly* a lie – the lamp hadn't done a thing.

Heidi clucked sympathetically. "Aw, sorry, kiddo. Maybe next time."

"Hmm, I think I'm done with lamps." Jennifer glanced back to where Pol had been hovering. He'd vanished, but beside her bed was a hat stand that *definitely* hadn't been there before.

"Actually," she continued hastily, faking a yawn, "I'm dead tired – "

"I bet, sweetie," Heidi said. She was about to say something else, but then she sniffed. Her face grew a bit green and she coughed. "Well, you sleep tight now."

Heidi's footsteps faded down the hall. Sighing with relief, Jennifer turned … and flinched. Pol was sitting *right* behind her.

"Argh!" she gasped. "You startled me! Anyway, what made you turn into a hat stand?"

"It's obvious!" Pol snapped back. "I didn't want to be caught!"

"Well, next time, pick something else! Who owns a hat stand? If Heidi had spotted you, she'd have known at once that something was off!" Jennifer paused. Pol was looking sad, which *wouldn't* help her get that free first wish. "Don't worry," she said. "What were you saying? You're Pol, the great and wise – "

"Yes," Pol grinned. "Pol, the great and wise Pooka."

"The what?"

"Pooka! You've never heard of a Pooka before? Well, we do all sorts, shape-shift, grant wishes – "

It was just what she wanted to hear. "You grant wishes! You're a jinn!"

"A what?"

"A jinn, you know, a powerful being who grants three wishes?"

"That's the one," said Pol. "Genie, innit? Three wishes."

Hmm, he didn't seem sure, *and* he got the name wrong, but Jennifer didn't worry about it. She'd planned this first conversation for a long time. If she was careful now, she could get *four* wishes.

"So," she said, casually, "if I wanted to win my sports day race tomorrow, you could do that?"

"Sure."

"I don't believe you."

Pol's glowing eyes blinked.

"O-K," he said, eventually. He began to wander around the room. "Nice place, this. A lot warmer than the last hovel I visited – "

"*You can't do it!*" said Jennifer, hoping to force Pol to prove himself without having to use up a wish. "You don't have enough power to make me win sports day."

Pol stared at her, his mouth a flat line. Finally, he shrugged. "All right," he said, "I'll do it. Sports day is tomorrow, right? That Casey normally wins, right?"

"Right," said Jennifer, amazed that Pol knew all this.

"I'm not surprised, she's *fast*," Pol agreed. "OK, so you'll win now."

"Really?" asked Jennifer, excitedly.

"Yep. Nobody will finish that race before you. Now, I must sleep."

"Sleep? You've just woken up after thousands of years!"

Pol shrugged. "You know when you spend all day doing nothing and it makes you feel tired ... I'll see you tomorrow."

"Wish me luck for sports day!" Jennifer said.

"You don't need luck," he said. "You've already cheated."

Ouch. Had she cheated? Her first encounter with a jinn hadn't quite been like she'd imagined. But still, as she got ready for bed, Jennifer grinned with joy. He was rude and scruffy, but Pol was what she'd been searching for. Her wish was his command!

Jennifer's first thought the next day was that she'd dreamed everything. But the biscuit tin was still on her bedroom floor, and when she knocked on the lid, a grumpy, sleepy voice answered. "Wassup?"

"Pol? It's Jennifer."

"What time is it?"

"It's eight o'clock."

"In the morning?! What's wrong with ya?! Go back to sleep!"

And that was all she could get out of him. It didn't matter.

Jennifer usually felt sick and very grumpy on big days. But today she guzzled down her breakfast and talked excitedly with Dad about the upcoming sports day. Later, at school, when Casey's sharp-tongued friend Sally-Ann said racing was a waste of time because everyone knew that Casey would win, Jennifer didn't get annoyed. She looked at the disheartened faces of the other racers on the starting line and had to fight back a smile. This race would be hers!

"Good luck, Jen."

That was Casey, in the lane next to her. She was the only other person who didn't look sick with worry. *But then why would you, when you're the fastest, most popular, richest girl in the school*, Jennifer thought. She didn't dislike Casey. It just felt unfair sometimes. She smiled back. "You too, Casey!" she said.

"READY!" the teacher roared. "SET! GO!"

Jennifer burst out from the starting line. At once, she felt the wind rush through her hair – she had never been this fast before! No one was in front of her, nobody was even close. She looked to see if her classmates were cheering her on and …

The crowd was strangely quiet. People weren't yelling – they weren't even smiling. Frowning, Jennifer slowed to a stop and looked back. And a nasty feeling turned her tummy.

The other racers were still at the starting line. They hadn't taken a single step.

"Are you OK, girls?" she heard a teacher say.

Casey looked utterly baffled. "I can't move," she said.

Sure enough, the entire row was rooted in their starting positions.

A chill ran through Jennifer's veins. *Nobody will finish the race before you*. That's what Pol had said. Surely, he hadn't meant this? One racer started to cry, and still they didn't budge. Would Jennifer have to complete the race before they could move? The thought made her cringe. Crossing the finish line when all your opponents were frozen at the start line was *not* a victory. She began to walk towards the finish line as casually as she could.

Sally-Ann's voice whispered from the sidelines. "Is Jennifer actually finishing the race? I can't believe it!"

It was the longest walk of her life. The moment Jennifer crossed the line, the other racers were released from their mysterious suspended state, flying forwards in a stumbling sprint. Her face red with embarrassment, Jennifer turned and jogged back to help. On the way she heard Sally-Ann again.

"That's the only way she'll ever beat Casey," she said.

Bonus

Bizarre sports day

STUDENTS STAND STOCK STILL AT STRANGE SCHOOL SPORTS DAY

Pupils, teachers and parents were shocked yesterday when the Girls Sprint Race – what some call the 'Event of the Year' – ended with only one contender finishing the race. Why? Because the other students couldn't move from the starting line.

"It's like they were stunned," their teacher said, "I was stunned!"

Nobody knew why the racers were frozen in place, although one parent suggested that this could be an event in next years sports day – the 'Standing Still Race'.

When asked how that race would end, however, the parent just walked away muttering that they "couldn't come up with everything."

Luckily, the racers were able to move soon after, and none of them suffered any lasting effects, though some of them were understandably upset. The winner of the race, Jennifer Jones, did not hang around to celebrate afterwards.

Chapter 3

"What were you thinking, Pol?!"

After that terrible race, it was the only question Jennifer wanted to ask him. But Pol seemed oblivious to his mistake.

"You should've said you wanted it to *look* fair," he said, blowing out his cheeks. "Things have to balance – you wanted to be a winner, so you needed nine other losers, catch my drift?"

"Catch your what?" Jennifer snapped. "And no, I didn't want nine losers, I – "

He was frustrating, this jinn. He twisted her words into terrible ideas.

"I'll be more careful what words I use for my first wish," she said eventually.

Pol stared at her. "Whatchoo mean, 'first wish'?" he demanded. "What was yer sports day, a polite request?"

"Ah," Jennifer said, feeling very pleased with herself. "Technically, I didn't 'wish'. You just did it."

Pol's eyes narrowed. She briefly wondered if jinn could punish cheeky children, but then a strange smile crossed his face. "OK," he said. "What do you wish?"

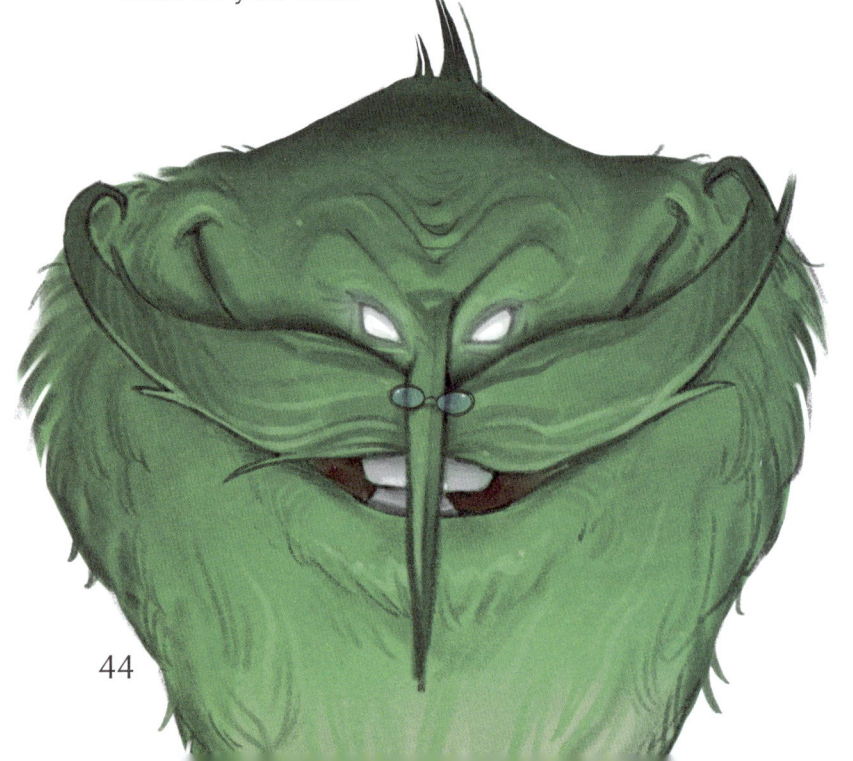

Jennifer grinned. Things were going her way at last! "My first wish is for an incredible birthday party, even better than – "

She trailed off. Pol was frowning.

"Oh, sorry, Jennifer," he said, not sounding sorry at all. "I'm an ancient spirit, you see. I only hear wishes if they're made in the proper way."

Jennifer gaped at him. "I don't know what you mean!"

"You don't?" Pol's mouth looked sad. His glowing eyes did not. "Shame. Normally I'd ignore the rules, but seeing as we're being careful with our words – "

"For my *second* wish – " Jennifer interrupted him through gritted teeth.

"I'm listening," Pol said. His mock-serious face was *infuriating*, but Jennifer had to concentrate.

"I want a perfect birthday party like Casey's, only better. I want it to be at a really posh restaurant where they put ketchup in little pots, and I want there to be a dancefloor and I want a famous celebrity to appear. I want everyone in my year to go, and I want them to think it's the best party ever, even Casey. That DOESN'T mean *their* birthdays have to be rubbish or anything like that."

OK, so with just two wishes left, Jennifer should have dropped the birthday party. She knew it wasn't as important as getting a new house, and she was supposed to be using her last wish to release Pol from the biscuit tin. But – and please don't judge her too harshly for this – at the last minute, she decided to take the 'Free Pol' wish away. She didn't do it deliberately, in the same way you don't set out to take the biggest piece of cake. It just sort of … happened. One minute, she was annoyed at Pol for the first wish. The next, she was asking for a birthday party, which meant … she wouldn't be able to free Pol after all.

"The best birthday party," Pol repeated, smiling. "I haven't been to a party in centuries."

"Oh." Jennifer paused. Pol wouldn't fit in at her perfect party. How could she get out of inviting him?

Luckily, Pol didn't ask. He smiled, a bit sadly maybe, and nodded. "The best birthday party it is. Just remember. Things have to balance."

She still didn't really know what that meant.

Pol was true to his word. The party was *spectacular*. There were origami napkins, little ketchup pots, and golden banners with HAPPY BIRTHDAY JENNIFER beneath magnificent balloon arches. After the meal – which everyone sat down for like grown-ups – the floor *opened up* to reveal a huge dancefloor! Jennifer had worried about the famous celebrity – what if Pol brought some old actor only her dad knew? But it was a singer they all *loved*, and Jennifer danced for *ages*.

At the end, Casey herself came up to her. "This is the best party ever!" she exclaimed. "I love the party bags!"

"Party bags?" Jennifer asked. Casey held one out. It was an old lamp, one of the many she had bought at the car boot sale, packed with small treats. At first, Jennifer was worried – she didn't want second-hand things at this posh party. But Casey was beaming.

"My own genie lamp!" she said. "Where did you get them? Online?"

"N-no," Jennifer said, stunned. "We go to the car boot sale sometimes."

"Amazing!"

It was one of those parties where nothing goes wrong and everyone leaves with a smile. At the end, Jennifer rushed up to Heidi and gave her a massive thank-you hug.

"That's OK," Heidi said, laughing. "You deserve it. I hope you didn't mind me giving the lamps as party bags? You said you wanted to get rid of them."

"It was perfect. I wouldn't change a thing."

"Great. I'll drop you home, and come back to help your dad wash the dishes, before he – "

"Wash the dishes?" Jennifer asked, frowning. "What do you mean?"

"Well, the party was a lot more than we could afford. Don't worry though, we got money off for doing the dishes, your dad got an extra nighttime job, and we sold the car, and … Jennifer, are you OK?"

Jennifer turned away, her heart pounding. She ran through the restaurant and through a door marked STAFF ONLY. The kitchen was packed with dirty dishes. Her dad was at the sink. He looked exhausted.

"Almost done, love!" he called.

Before she could reply, Jennifer caught a familiar smell coming from behind a door. She hurried through it, and found Pol.

"Happy birthday!" he cheered. Then he saw her anger and his face fell.

"My dad is washing the dishes," Jennifer spat. *"They've sold their car."*

"Well, yeah," said Pol, confused. "I mean, it's not a cheap party, is it?"

"THAT'S WHY I WISHED FOR IT!" Jennifer shouted. "I WANTED A PARTY BETTER THAN CASEY'S! HER DAD DIDN'T HAVE TO WASH THE DISHES, DID HE?!"

Pol blinked those glowing eyes. "Well, nah," he said. "But Casey's dad is richer than yours."

"You want to know why I wanted to make this my *first* wish?" Jennifer seethed. "Why I wanted *two* more wishes afterwards? It was because on my third wish, the one you *stole* from me, I was going to release you from the lamp."

"I don't live in a la—"

"THE BISCUIT TIN, THEN! I was going to set you free, and we could've been friends."

"Who said I needed setting free?"

Jennifer took a moment to reply. It didn't make sense. Pol was a jinn, wasn't he? He *had* to give wishes until he was set free, didn't he? But in truth, she didn't care. She was so *angry*. Angry that her dad was tired, angry that another wish had turned sour. Angry because things were unfair.

"For my last wish," she said, in a trembling voice, "I want *everything* Casey has. I want the biggest house, the most money, the most friends – "

"Hold up, Jen – " Pol looked worried. But Jennifer wasn't listening.

"I want to win all the races and get top marks in tests. And I don't want my dad or Heidi to *ever* have to wash the dishes again. That's my wish, Pol. Then you can go back to your biscuit tin. I don't want to see you anymore."

Bonus

Party checklist

Jennifer Jones's checklist for the best birthday party ever

ketchup in little pots

origami napkins

balloons

food treats

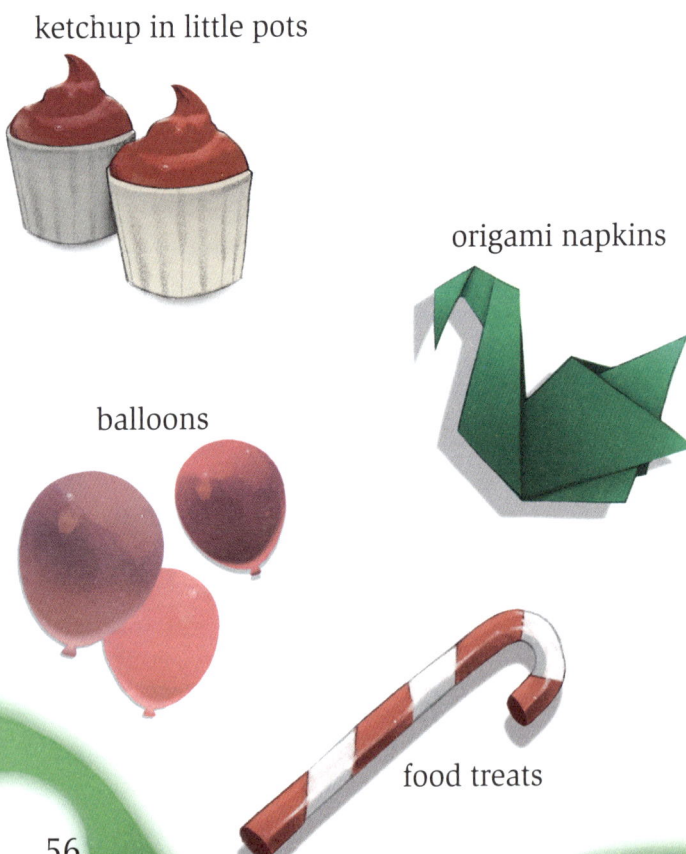

dancefloor

music

games

presents

people I care about

Chapter 4

Jennifer Jones woke up. The sun was shining through a gap in her thick curtains. She stretched and rolled over. Then, she rolled over again. (Her bed was a lot bigger than before.)

Getting out, her feet touched thick, luxurious carpet. Jennifer yawned and looked around. Her room was *massive*. In the corner, a TV hung from the wall, gaming consoles stacked beneath it!

As she walked to her wardrobe, the doors opened automatically. The clothes inside were cool, designer, and all brand new. She got changed and went downstairs.

Her dad and Heidi were in the kitchen, eating at an enormous table.

"Morning, Dad," Jennifer said, but her dad waved at her to be quiet. He was speaking into an earphone, she realised.

"So we'll keep the search open," he was saying. "She can't hide forever. Keep me informed."

Wondering who he was talking about, Jennifer looked at Heidi. She was on her phone too, playing a game.

"Morning, Heidi," she said, with a smile. "Any bagels today?"

"Heya, sweetie," Heidi said, not looking up. "Er, I don't know, ask one of the staff. Don't you want them to make you pancakes like normal?"

"You know what?" Jennifer said, with a grin. "Pancakes would be *perfect*."

The morning went on being incredible. After receiving a stack of the fluffiest pancakes imaginable, Jennifer took a *limousine* to school!

When she arrived, her friends – and there were *lots* of them – were waiting for her.

"Is this a welcome parade or something?!" she said, with a smile, and they all laughed.

Even her lessons were better! Jennifer got ten out of ten on a Maths test, even though she was *sure* she'd messed up at least two of the questions. Her teacher was so impressed, he gave her *Star of the Week*, and it was not even halfway through!

"You've worked so hard, Jennifer," he said. "You're *already* the star."

Jennifer flushed with pride, and if Pol's words ran through her mind just a little bit (*You don't need luck. You've already cheated …*) then she ignored them.

At breaktime, she didn't even get time to play, because so many people were hurrying up to thank her for her birthday party the night before.

And if she thought about the cost of the party, of Dad washing up endless dishes and Heidi looking exhausted, Jennifer ignored how it made her feel.

The only strange thing about this amazing new life was Casey. She was nowhere to be seen. Jennifer asked Casey's best friend, Sally-Ann, where she might be, and expected a mean comment back, but instead Sally-Ann looked away nervously.

"I don't know where Casey is," was all she would say.

It shouldn't have really mattered. Why would Casey need to be there for Jennifer to enjoy her day? But still, it gnawed at her, even when her team won at hockey (after Jennifer scored the winning goal, of course), and *even* when the Head gave her a Special Award for picking up a drinks bottle that she had dropped. Only at the very end of her best school day ever, did Jennifer overhear something that explained why Casey was missing.

The trouble was, it explained everything else as well.

It happened after the final school bell. Jennifer was walking out to the gates, with her friends all telling her how *amazing* the goal she scored in hockey was, when suddenly she remembered something.

"My coat!" she yelled. "I forgot my coat!"

"I'll get it!" Sally-Ann said quickly.

"You will?!" Jennifer said, surprised. Even stranger, a boy in their class, Zefran, also turned back.

"I'll help Sally-Ann, in case she can't find it," he said.

"Er – thanks," Jennifer said, *very* bemused now. She stood there and waited, for so long that her friends ran out of things to say about her hockey goal and talked instead about her Maths test – *"I've never seen anyone work out Maths problems like that!"*

Then, with a sudden flash, she remembered to check inside her bag. She opened it … and groaned. "Argh, I'm such a dingbat! My coat was in here all along! I'll go and tell the others they don't need to look."

"I can do that, Jennifer," one of the other girls began to say. But, to be honest, Jennifer was getting a bit tired of listening to stories about how great she was.

"It's fine," she said firmly. "It won't take long," and she jogged back inside before any of her friends could argue. She was just outside her classroom when she heard Sally-Ann's voice. To Jennifer's amazement, the girl sounded absolutely petrified.

"Where is it? I can't find it anywhere. Why did I offer to find it? I'm so stupid!"

"Don't worry," Zefran replied, although he sounded worried himself. "It'll show up. If not, we'll just offer to buy her a new one."

"We can't afford that," Sally-Ann said. "Have you seen how expensive her clothes are? We'll just have to stay here till we find it. Oh, why did I even offer! I'm such a suck-up."

Jennifer, listening, was about to hurry in and say not to worry, that of course this wasn't Sally-Ann's fault. But then she added something that stopped her cold.

"Jennifer Jones hates me. I'm going to have to run away like Casey."

Jennifer snuck home, leaving her 'friends' behind. Suddenly, everything made horrible sense. The way everyone laughed at her jokes. The way her teacher awarded her *Star of the Week* on a Tuesday. Even her dad's phone call that morning – "She can't hide forever" – suddenly made sense. They were all terrified of Jennifer Jones, and for good reason. After all, when Casey annoyed Jennifer Jones, she was forced to run away.

With the nasty feeling she'd made a terrible mistake, Jennifer rushed through her front door and up the stairs.

On the way up to her room, she passed framed newspaper articles that hung from the wall. The headlines told her what had happened.

The more Jennifer saw, the worse she felt. Finally, she understood Pol's warnings about balance. He couldn't just 'magic' Jennifer's perfect life. There was one way he could give her lots of money *and* countless fawning friends *and* gold medals *and* top marks on every test, and that was to make everyone else terrified of her.

She thought about all the smiles she'd received that day, all the questions she'd got 'right', all the jokes everyone had laughed at. Now they all left a bad taste in her mouth.

"Pol," she muttered, and sped up the stairs, bursting through the door and into …

… but this wasn't her bedroom, not the one from her real life. There was no biscuit tin on the floor, no second-hand lamps, no homemade toybox. This massive, modern bedroom had everything she'd ever wanted … and now she didn't want it at all.

"Pol," Jennifer said again. There was a lump in her throat, and her heart was racing. She was trapped in a strange world, and everybody was afraid of her; it was all so fake. And the only person who could fix it was gone.

The tears began to fall.

Bonus

Map of Jennifer's town

Chapter 5

Sometimes, crying is like a shower, washing away your worries, fears and shame. When Jennifer had finished, she was still in her strange big bedroom, and Pol was still missing. But her mind felt clearer.

There was one place she hadn't looked: her *old* flat.

She crept out of the mansion. This wasn't as easy as it might seem, as there were a lot of staff desperate to impress her.

"I've finished stacking the dishwasher, Jen!"

"I've put all your clothes away, Jennifer!"

Normally, Jennifer would have been delighted – these were two chores *she* had to do, and the idea that somebody else would do them seemed great. Now, though, she saw the worried way they told her, as if at any moment she might tell them off. It made her feel even worse.

"Er, great," she said awkwardly. "Why don't you have the day off, then?"

At last, Jennifer was out of the mansion and racing down the hill to her old flat. It's funny how things seem so much better when you've seen how bad they could be. On the way down, she passed the familiar pastry shop where Heidi would always wave to Jennifer when she walked by. She passed the green where the car boot sale took place, and imagined Old Shay's table with all its strange antique treasures.

Did Jennifer Jones go to a car boot sale in *this* reality? Probably not. Even her school, where that day, Jennifer had been made *Star of the Week* and got top marks in a test, didn't seem half as friendly as before. Passing it now, Jennifer missed yesterday, when she *knew* her friends were her real friends and not just afraid of her, and when any praise from the teacher had felt real and hard-earned.

Soon it became too much to take. Jennifer picked up speed, running faster and faster, until the whole town became a blur and all she wanted was to see her old flat again. *Please let it still be there*, she thought, *our lovely home with the squeaky gate and the temperamental doorbell and the rattly windows …*

It was. Jennifer sped up the moment she saw it, like she'd found an old friend. The gate *still* squeaked when she opened it, and the doorbell still didn't work, so she had to knock on the frosted glass of the front door. A figure came to the door, and for one moment, Jennifer imagined that it was Heidi.

Then the door opened.

"Hello?"

It wasn't Heidi.

It was Casey's mum.

Jennifer didn't really know Casey's mum, but she did know that she was very friendly, and that she normally looked glamorous, like she'd just come from a film shoot or a fancy party. Today, however, her mouth was turned down in an unhappy scowl, and when her tired eyes took in Jennifer, they widened for a moment … before narrowing with dislike. She wasn't just shocked to see Jennifer. She was *angry*.

"Mrs, er – " Jennifer suddenly realised she didn't know Casey's second name. "Can I come in? I'm so sorry, honestly, about *everything*. But I think there might be something in my – in Casey's room that will make everything better."

Casey's mum stared at her in disbelief. "In Casey's room?" she said.

"Please," Jennifer begged. "I know it seems absurd. But something is *very* wrong about this town. It isn't how things are supposed to be. *Please*, can you let me in, just for five minutes?"

Casey's mum stared at her. She clearly wanted to tell her to go away, or something like that. But something in Jennifer's face must have showed that she was telling the truth, because instead Casey's mum gave a quick little nod, and Jennifer ran in.

Casey's bedroom was the same as her own bedroom: the wardrobe on one side, the toybox on another, her bed in the corner.

Jennifer burst in, and for a moment, it was such a shock to be in her old bedroom that all she could do was look around wildly. Then she looked at the floor, and her heart sank.

There wasn't a biscuit tin to be seen anywhere.

"Pol," Jennifer murmured, fighting back a sob. She had been so sure the tin would be here. Now she was trapped in this horrible life, and even worse, she had trapped everyone else in it too.

She was about to turn away, when she heard the slightest sniffle. She froze. The sound had come from beneath the bed. "Casey?" she whispered, and crouched down. Underneath, the bed was stuffed with bags and boxes, but there was a figure hidden behind them, facing away from her.

"Casey, I am *so* sorry. I didn't think this would happen. I just … I just saw my life as unfair. I didn't realise there were lots of things I was lucky to have. But I promise. Even if I can't wish my way out of this mess, I'm going to make things better. Please, you have to believe me!"

It was the most meaningful speech Jennifer could remember making. But the figure still didn't speak, and eventually, she sighed. She was about to say goodbye and sorry again, when the figure coughed.

That's when she sniffed an unpleasant smell.

"It stinks in here," the figure said. "Was that you?"

"Pol!" Jennifer said joyfully. She dragged the bags out of the way as quickly as she could and threw herself under the bed. By then, Pol had turned to face her, his face sad and sorrowful.

"I did everything you asked," he said. "But the fastest and the smartest and the richest *and* the most popular? It's hard to balance out."

Jennifer nodded. "I'm so sorry, Pol. Sorry for not inviting you to my birthday party. Sorry for telling you that I wouldn't set you free. Sorry for saying I didn't want to see you anymore."

Pol shook his head. "You were upset," he said. "Maybe I shouldn't have been giving those wishes at all. But sometimes, it's a bit lonely being cooped up in a tin. I thought that if I gave you the wishes you asked for, then maybe you would want to be my friend."

Jennifer took a deep breath. Pol's mouth was a wobbly line, trembling as though he was holding back tears himself. *Right then*, she thought. If she had a wish left, then she would wish for him to feel better, so that she didn't feel so bad. But, she was starting to realise, things would never be as simple as that.

"I'm sorry," she said again. "I really am."

Pol smiled. It was a sad smile. But it was a smile all the same.

"Thank you, Jennifer Jones. That means a lot. And … maybe you were right about your first wish not being a wish. You never *actually* said 'I wish to win the race', after all. Perhaps … perhaps for your final wish, you'd like everything back the way it was?"

Jennifer gulped. It was what she wanted, more than anything else. She nodded, unable to speak.

Everything went hazy.

Then everything disappeared.

Chapter 6

Jennifer Jones woke up. Her mattress was lumpy, and her room felt small. She smiled and leaped out of bed.

"Pol?" she said. "Pol, you did it!"

There was no answer. The biscuit tin, Pol's metal home, had disappeared.

Jennifer scoured her bedroom for the tin, looking in her wardrobe, in the half-empty toybox, even under her bed. But her heart knew the truth even before her head did. Pol was gone. It made sense, in some ways. Pol had asked her if she wanted everything to go back to the way it was before, and she'd said yes. But before, she didn't have him. It hurt, like a friend had moved away.

It was early in the morning, but Heidi was already up when Jennifer went to the kitchen, laying out pastries for breakfast.

"Morning, Jennifer," she said cheerfully, and Jennifer was so happy to see her that she forgot about Pol for the moment. "Want a croissant?"

"Thanks, Heidi," Jennifer said, with a grin, and took a bite. "Mmmm, better than pancakes."

Heidi chuckled. "I don't know about that. Maybe if we had a chef to make the pancakes for us."

Jennifer thought of the cooks and cleaners in the mansion, running around scared of her. She shuddered. "Urgh, no thank you," she said. "Your pastries are way better, Heidi."

Perhaps it pleased Heidi, saying that, because her cheeks went red and she quickly busied herself getting ready for work, and gave Jennifer an extra-big hug before leaving.

"Car boot on Sunday?" she asked, and Jennifer nodded. She couldn't be happier to be home again.

School was nice too. Not for any big reason, more just one of those quiet days when Jennifer finished her work and played with her friends, who were all glad to see her just because they were glad to see her.

It was just after break, however, when Jennifer realised that Pol hadn't *quite* succeeded in making everything revert to the way it was. When they got back to class, their teacher said that there was going to be a repeat of the girl's race, seeing as the last one had to be abandoned.

"Even though Jennifer *still* tried to win it," Sally-Ann pointed out, and for a moment Jennifer was horrified. *That still happened?!* she thought. But then, before she even had time to defend herself, Casey was putting up her hand.

"It wasn't like that, Sally-Ann," she said. "How could it be Jennifer's fault? And anyway, she came to help us. You shouldn't be so mean."

Sally-Ann didn't say much after that.

The race that afternoon was one of Jennifer's best yet. Casey won, but just by a bit, and Jennifer was faster than ever. She gave Casey a hug to say well done, and made a secret vow to practise running all year – it wouldn't take much for her to win the next race!

Her wish to have things back exactly as they used to be, hadn't entirely come true. Jennifer realised this when she saw her toybox empty of all the old lamps she didn't know what to do with. Dad still had to work an extra job to pay for Jennifer's expensive birthday party. Neither he nor Heidi seemed to mind, but Jennifer felt very guilty, and tried to find ways to help. She also missed Pol, even though he'd been smelly, and sometimes rude, and he had a nasty habit of making her see the other side of what she wanted.

◠◠◠

Sunday came around quickly, and Heidi was as good as her word, taking Jennifer to the car boot sale.

"I suppose you'll be going to Old Shay's table again," she chuckled, but Jennifer shook her head.

"Not today," she said. "There's a present I want to buy first."

Jennifer spent a good hour looking around for it. Something completely unexpected happened during that time: she ran into Casey!

"Heya, Jen!" Casey called out. "Thank you so much for telling me about this car boot – I love it."

"You do?" said Jennifer, and Casey started to talk about all the amazing things she had seen for sale, strange valuables that seemed to be from a mystical land. She was interrupted, however, by her mum, who was marvelling at the clothes she'd found at a nearby stall.

"Casey!" she called over. "Casey! Come look at these tops, they're designer!"

Casey looked embarrassed. It was the first time Jennifer had ever seen her uncomfortable in a place, like she didn't know how to fit in.

"My, er, mum's a bit excited too," she said awkwardly.

"Yeah, I get that," Jennifer said. "You should see my dad with the Christmas decorations. It's mortifying."

Before they parted, Jennifer promised to tell Casey all about the treasures she found at the car boot at school on Monday. Then she continued looking for the important present. It took Jennifer ages to find, but when she did, she was delighted. She thanked the seller, and hurried across the car boot sale with it on her shoulder.

"Not you again!" Old Shay began, as Jennifer walked up to him. Then he saw what Jennifer was lugging around, and broke off.

It was a fold-up chair.

"I got this for you," she said. "So you can rest your bad feet."

"Flippin' heck," Old Shay said softly. She handed it over and he sat down on it, looking around the car boot. A big smile spread across his face, and he waggled his legs. "My feet! My bad feet! They feel better already. What am I supposed to moan about now?! Thank you, Jennifer."

"You're welcome," Jennifer said, with a grin. She thought about telling Old Shay all about Pol and the biscuit tin, but it seemed so unbelievable now. Instead, she looked around Old Shay's table.

"Tell me you're not looking for another lamp," he groaned, but she shook her head.

"Nah," she said, "I'm just browsing. Although … what's that?"

It was an old map, yellow and curled. Jennifer lifted it up and looked at it more closely. She could have sworn the streets on the map looked like the streets around her house. In one street, an 'X' marked a particular spot.

"It's a treasure map," she said, with a surge of excitement. "Isn't it?"

"Heaven help me," Old Shay groaned. But he shot her a sly glance with eyes as grey as the skies above. "It's three pounds. You wouldn't happen to have that on you now?"

Jennifer handed over the money, feeling more excited than ever. If she found the treasure, her dad wouldn't have to do the extra night work. They could buy back the car. Maybe there would be a bit left over as well … although she was only really thinking about the first two things. She was about to pick up the map, when Old Shay held up a hand.

"Hang on a minute," he said. "You'll damage it, lugging it about like that. Fold it up, and I'll find something to put it in."

"Like what, Shay?" she asked. And the old man's eyes twinkled.

"Like a biscuit tin."

Bonus

Pol's favourite wishes

I wish my little brother had to do the dishes every day and they *never* ended.

I wish … for the strongest arms EVER, and the fastest legs EVER.

I wish … I was as tall as the world's tallest building.

I wish … for a never-ending sweet jar.

I wish … for unlimited wishes.

About the author

Did you always want to be an author?

Colm Field

Honestly? I didn't think of it as being a possible job for a long time! But I always loved coming up with stories. When I started to write on my phone, I could do it anywhere, whenever I had five minutes free, and it became a brilliant habit that helped me sort through my thoughts. I could think about the things I was worried about and enjoy the funny things that happened to me all over again. I feel so lucky now that I get paid to write, although I would have kept on writing, no matter what.

What's your favourite thing about being an author?

There are two best bits for me. The first is when I have an idea for a story, and start to imagine what would happen next. The second is when I have written the story, and gone over it again and again, until it's something that I feel proud of.

How did you come up with the idea for this story?

I honestly love car boot sales and finding old things that *might* be treasure, or at least have their own story. But car boot sales can have all sorts in them and it occurred to me that if I ever *did* find a genie there, they probably wouldn't be the genie I expected …

Do you have a favourite character in this book?

I like all of them. They all feel like their own people that were alive before I even started writing them. But Pol makes me laugh the most.

Are any of the characters based on real people?

All the characters are based a bit on somebody I know. Casey is DEFINITELY based on those people who are so good at everything you get annoyed, even though they might be nice people. Also, Sally-Ann. I work on building sites, and everyone on building sites likes to shout their opinion about everything, me included. Casey's mate Sally-Ann is like that person who shouts on the building site, and like them, she is extra annoying because she is probably more right than Jennifer would like to admit. Oh, and Jennifer Jones herself ... I have three children and can remember plenty of moments where they have acted just like her, dug themselves a deeper hole trying to tidy up the mess they've made. I've been there myself, and believe me when I say this: it's not the boo-boo that makes you, it's finally accepting what you need to do to fix it.

Does anything relate to your own experiences?

I think when things are a bit tough, everyone looks at other people's lives with envy. I'm guilty of that, even though when the sun comes out again, I realise that there are lots of things to be thankful for.

Do you have a favourite part of the story?

All the bits where Jennifer and Pol are bickering make me smile.

What do you hope readers will get from the book?

A fun story! And a reminder to appreciate the good things in your life. Oh, and please please please, if you would write a different story yourself then DO. Nobody else can create the tales you could come up with, I promise you that. Next time you've got five minutes and a pen, a tablet, or even just your brain, spend that time on a story you would like to read yourself.

About the illustrator

Did you always want to be an illustrator?

Tom Bonson

Yes, I grew up surrounded by creativity – both my parents were illustrators so it rubbed off on me early. I remember sitting at the kitchen table with them, doodling while they worked. It never felt like 'work', more like magic being made on the page. Seeing them turn blank paper into whole worlds was inspiring, and it gave me the confidence that drawing could actually be a career, not just a hobby.

How did you get into illustrating?

I studied Fine Art and then Illustration at university, and things took off from there! I experimented with different mediums before finally deciding on digital, but learning to draw the traditional way really helped. At university, I connected with other artists and writers, which gave me opportunities to collaborate. Those first projects taught me how to adapt my style depending on the story, which is a big part of professional illustration.

What was your favourite scene to illustrate?

The town scene. I got to pack it with quirky little details, such as a market stall and little signs.

What was the most challenging thing about illustrating this book?

Getting the emotional moments just right without losing the charm or humour was a challenge. Balancing comedy with sincerity can be tricky – I wanted readers to laugh, but also feel the heart of the story. Sometimes that meant redrawing the same character expression a dozen times until it felt honest.

Do you use pens and paints or do you work digitally?

Digitally – I love the flexibility it gives – if you make a mistake, you can just click the 'undo' button! But I still sketch by hand first, because there's an energy in pencil lines that I like to capture before refining on screen.

Which character in the book did you identify with the most?

Jennifer, because she's slightly awkward but brave. This makes her very human. I think we've all had moments of doubt like that. Drawing Jennifer was a reminder that courage doesn't mean being fearless, it means being scared but doing the thing anyway.

Which character was the most fun to draw?

The farty genie! He's unpredictable, chaotic, and a little gross in the funniest way. Every sketch of him made me laugh, and I think readers will feel that energy too.

What would you wish for if a genie gave you three wishes?

World peace, crisps, and smiles and laughter for all.

Book chat

How do you think Jennifer changes during this story?

Do any of the other characters change?

What's your favourite part of the story?

Does this book remind you of any other stories?

Do you think this book has a villain? If so, who?

Do you think this book would make a good film? Why, or why not?

What do you think will happen to Jennifer next?

If you could talk to a character from the book, who would you choose? What would you ask?

Who would you recommend this book to and why?

Book challenge:

What three wishes would you make if you met Pol? What might happen?

Published by Collins
An imprint of HarperCollins*Publishers*

The News Building
1 London Bridge Street
London
SE1 9GF
UK

Macken House
39/40 Mayor Street Upper
Dublin 1
D01 C9W8
Ireland

Text © Colm Field 2025
Design and illustrations © HarperCollins*Publishers* Limited 2025

10 9 8 7 6 5 4 3 2 1

ISBN 978-0-00-876783-9

All rights reserved. No part of this publication may be reproduced, stored in a retrieval system, or transmitted in any form by any means, electronic, mechanical, photocopying, recording or otherwise, without the prior written permission of the Publisher or a licence permitting restricted copying in the United Kingdom issued by the Copyright Licensing Agency Ltd, 5th Floor, Shackleton House, 4 Battle Bridge Lane, London SE1 2HX.

Without limiting the exclusive rights of any author, contributor or the publisher of this publication, any unauthorised use of this publication to train generative artificial intelligence (AI) technologies is expressly prohibited. HarperCollins also exercise their rights under Article 4(3) of the Digital Single Market Directive 2019/790 and expressly reserve this publication from the text and data mining exception.

British Library Cataloguing-in-Publication Data
A catalogue record for this publication is available from the British Library.

Download the teaching notes and word cards to accompany this book at:
http://littlewandle.org.uk/signupfluency/

Get the latest Collins Big Cat news at
collins.co.uk/collinsbigcat

Author: Colm Field
Illustrator: Tom Bonson (Illustration X)
Publisher: Laura White
Product managers: Caroline Green and Holly Woolnough
Series editor: Charlotte Raby
Development editor: Catherine Baker
Commissioning editor: Caroline Green
Project manager: Emily Hooton
Copyeditor: Sally Byford
Proofreader: Catherine Dakin
Cover designer: Sarah Finan
Typesetter: 2Hoots Publishing Services Ltd
Production controller: Katharine Willard

Printed in the UK.

MIX
Paper | Supporting responsible forestry
FSC™ C007454

This book contains FSC™ certified paper and other controlled sources to ensure responsible forest management.

For more information visit: www.harpercollins.co.uk/green

Made with responsibly sourced paper and vegetable ink

Scan to see how we are reducing our environmental impact.